Snap books® Babysitter's Backpack

You're IN CHARGE

Basic Rules Every BABYSITTER Needs to Know

by Melissa Higgins

Consultant:
Lyn Horning
Assistant Director, Better Kid Care
Penn State University
University Park, Pennsylvania

CAPSTONE PRESS
a capstone imprint

Snap Books are published by Capstone Press,
1710 Roe Crest Drive, North Mankato, Minnesota 56003
www.capstonepub.com

Library of Congress Cataloging-in-Publication Data
Higgins, Melissa, 1953- author.
You're in charge : basic rules every babysitter needs to know / by Melissa Higgins.
     pages cm. — (Babysitter's backpack)
Includes index.
  Summary: "Discusses basic information about babysitting, including basic childcare"—
Provided by publisher.
  Audience: Grades 4 to 6.
  ISBN 978-1-4914-0764-6 (library binding) — ISBN 978-1-4914-0768-4 (eBook pdf)
1. Babysitting—Juvenile literature. 2. Safety education—Juvenile literature. I. Title. II.
Title: I am in charge.
  HQ769.5.H544 2015
  649.10248—dc23
                                    2014012068

Editorial Credits
Abby Colich, editor; Juliette Peters, designer; Tracy Cummins, media researcher;
Laura Manthe, production specialist

Photo Credits
Alamy: © Catchlight Visual Services, 3 Left, 14, 17, © Radius Images, 5 Top; Capstone Press: Karon Dubke, 3 Right, 7, 9, 13, 15 Top, 18, 19, 22, 23, 25 Bottom, 27 Top; Getty Images: Hero Images, 10, lostinbids, 26; iStockphotos: © vgajic, 2 Right, 11 Top; Shutterstock: BlueOrange Studio, 6, Denis Cristo, 5 Bottom, 11 Bottom, 15 Bottom, 24, 25 Top, 27 Bottom, 28 Bottom, Cover, GWImages, 8, Lena S, 16, Natykach Nataliia, Valentijn Tempels, 21, Veerachai Viteeman, Design Element; SuperStock: Fancy Collection, 12, Kwame Zikomo, 4, 2 Left

Printed in the United States of America in North Mankato, Minnesota
032014   008087CGF14

Page 4   Page 11

Table of Contents

Being a Responsible Leader

You need to earn a little money. You like kids. Or maybe your parents need you to watch a younger sibling for a few hours. Why not try babysitting? Babysitting is a fun and rewarding job. But caring for children first requires responsibility and preparation.

A responsible and prepared babysitter always knows:

- babysitting basics, such as feeding, diapering, and bathing
- the backgrounds of each child, such as health issues and food allergies, and how to handle them
- how to get in touch with the child's parents or guardians
- where emergency supplies, such as fire extinguishers and flashlights, are located
- the house rules and parents' expectations for you and their children
- simple first aid and when and where to call for help in an emergency
- to keep her full attention on the children and never leave children unattended

The more prepared you are, the more you'll be able to relax. You'll be able to have more fun with the children you're babysitting.

What Should You Do quiz questions throughout will help you know if you're ready to be a great babysitter. You can look up the answers on page 28.

Qualities of a Great Babysitter

Leadership is one of the most important qualities of a great babysitter. Children need to understand you're in charge. When you're an effective leader, you build trust and earn the respect of both children and their parents.

Role modeling: Demonstrate the behavior you want from the children you babysit. If you want them to have a good attitude, always smile and show enthusiasm.

Respect: Respect your employer and the children in your care. Follow all household rules and routines. It also means respecting people as individuals, even if they are different from you.

Communication: When talking with children, use words and sentences they can understand. Show you're listening by sitting or kneeling so you are at eye level with the child.

Making decisions and taking action: Being in charge sometimes means making fast decisions and taking action. Watch for situations that might need your help. Ask yourself exactly what the problem is and what would be the best solution.

Caring: Good babysitters enjoy being around and taking care of children. Show you care by being friendly. But don't try to be "cool" and let the children do whatever they want. Children behave best with structure and limits.

Getting Started

You think you have all the right qualities to be a great babysitter. Before you start looking for a job, make sure you've got the following points covered.

Get educated. Take babysitting classes and first-aid training.

Get your parents' approval. Know their rules and expectations for when, how often, and who you babysit.

Know your limits. Does caring for a newborn or a child with special needs make you nervous? What ages are you comfortable babysitting? Don't take a job that's not a good fit. Will babysitting conflict with your schoolwork or after school activities? Know how often you feel comfortable babysitting.

Find clients. Spread the word through family, friends, and neighbors that you're interested in babysitting.

Interview the family. When a new family asks you to babysit, you may want to jump at the opportunity. An interview lets you and the family figure out if you're a good match. Take a trusted adult or older sibling with you if you're going to meet a new family.

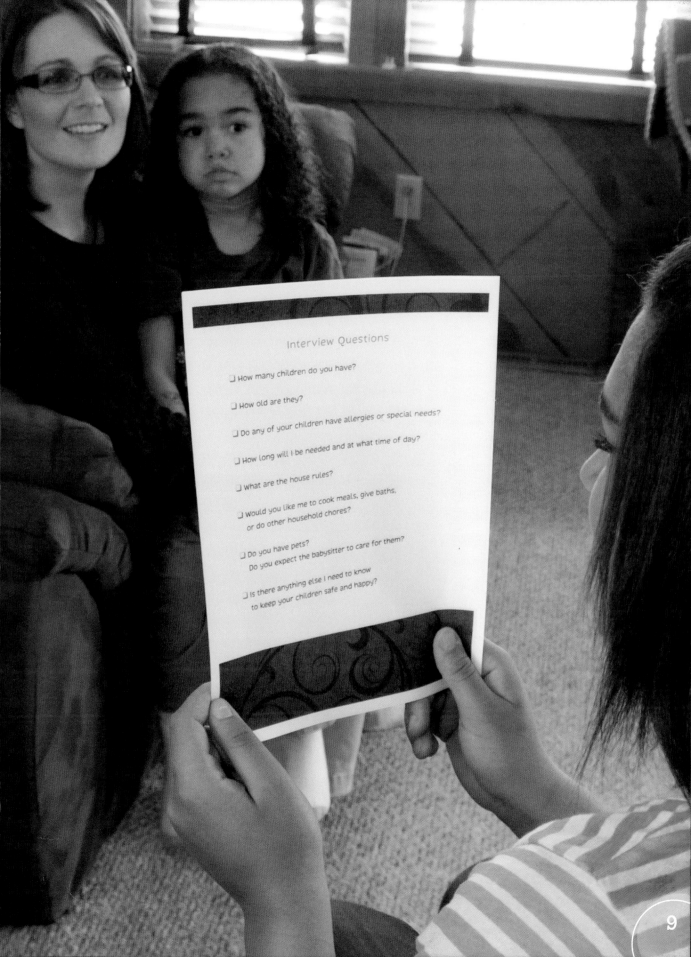

Interview Questions

☐ How many children do you have?

☐ How old are they?

☐ Do any of your children have allergies or special needs?

☐ How long will I be needed and at what time of day?

☐ What are the house rules?

☐ Would you like me to cook meals, give baths, or do other household chores?

☐ Do you have pets? Do you expect the babysitter to care for them?

☐ Is there anything else I need to know to keep your children safe and happy?

CHAPTER 2

Child Care Basics: Safety and Routines

Safety is always your first priority when babysitting. Pay attention to what's happening around you and use your common sense. Stick to the rules and routines you have discussed with parents.

Safety

Before you perform any kind of child care, make sure you understand and can perform basic emergency procedures. Take a basic first-aid class. Know when and whom to call in an emergency.

Be Aware of Your Surroundings

Remember the key rules in babysitting. Pay attention and never leave children alone! Be aware of what's going on around you. Are there toys scattered around that a child could trip on? Are there small objects nearby that a toddler could choke on? Paying attention to these things will keep kids safe and happy.

What Should You Do?

A friend invites you to a sleepover for her birthday, but you already promised your neighbor you would babysit. You should ...

A Get your brother to babysit for you.

B Cancel the babysitting job. The neighbor will understand once you explain.

C Decline the sleepover invitation and go to your babysitting job.

D Do neither. Making tough decisions is stressful!

Know the Routines and Rules

Children are happiest when they follow their normal routines. Discuss children's routines and preferences with parents at the beginning of each job. You should know:

- What meals or snacks should children have? What foods are OK to eat?
- How much TV or electronics time is allowed? At what times?
- What TV shows are children allowed to watch? What video games are they allowed to play?
- What other activities are OK?
- Do the children need baths? What are the instructions for this?
- When is bedtime? What is the children's bedtime routine?

A parent is likely to write down some of the things you need to know while you're babysitting. It might look something like this.

We will be at the Johnsons until 10:30 p.m.

and will be home by 11:00 p.m.

The Johnsons' home phone is 555-8793

or call my cell at 601-555-0511.

The kids have had dinner.

They can have apples or microwave popcorn for a snack

but not too close to bedtime.

No TV after 8:00 p.m.

and absolutely no video games after 7:30 p.m.

Bedtime is 8:30 p.m. but no later than 9:00 p.m.

Their pajamas are on their beds.

Make sure they brush their teeth.

Please give Sanya her medication.

The bottle is on her dresser.

One teaspoon before bed.

In an emergency, our address is 1072 Elm Street.

If you can't reach us call Grandma Sally at 702-555-4489.

CHAPTER 3

Caring for Infants and Toddlers

Dirty diapers. Thrown food. Keeping up with a 2-year-old. Caring for infants and toddlers can be messy and hectic. But it can also be fun when you're prepared and know what to expect.

Picking Up and Holding

Keep in mind that some children like to be held and others don't. Ask parents if their infant or toddler likes to be held. Respect each child's preference.

Infants: When holding an infant under 6 months old, always support the head, neck, and back. The child will feel more secure if you hold him close to your body.

Toddlers: Toddlers can be heavy. Make sure you're strong enough to give the child full support. Bend your knees and lift the child under the arms. Support the child with one arm under the bottom and your other arm supporting the back.

Sleep

Infants and toddlers do not always go to sleep easily and may cry. Ask parents in advance about their child's bedtime routine. Ask what to do when a child cries or has trouble falling asleep.

Sleep Safety Tips

Don't forget these safety tips when putting an infant or toddler to sleep in a crib.

❏ Be sure to remove any objects from an infant's crib, including pillows, stuffed animals, or other toys.
❏ Lay an infant face up on her back, unless a parent instructs you to lay the infant on her side. (In this case, have the parent show you exactly how to position her.)
❏ If the parents want you to cover their child with a blanket, tuck the bottom end of the blanket under the crib mattress. Then bring the blanket up to cover the child up to her chest.

Feeding

If you are asked to feed or prepare a meal for an infant or toddler, here are a few things to remember.

Bottle Feeding: Heat the bottle by holding it under warm running water. Never warm a baby's bottle in a microwave. Make sure it's not too hot by shaking a drop onto your wrist. Hold the baby so her head is supported and higher than the rest of her body. Tip the bottle so the nipple is always full of liquid. The baby will arch her back or push the nipple out of her mouth when she needs a break or is finished. Wait a few minutes, then touch the nipple to her lips to see if she wants more. Don't force a baby to eat more than she wants. After feeding, put a cloth over your shoulder. Hold the baby against your shoulder. Gently but firmly pat the infant's back until you hear a burp.

Spoon Feeding: Sit the baby in a highchair and fasten the safety straps. Put a little food on a baby spoon. Hold the spoon near the baby's mouth, and wait for the child to open his mouth. Put the food toward the middle of the baby's mouth. It's OK if he spits it out. Don't force him to eat.

Feeding Toddlers: Toddlers will likely use their fingers to eat. Be sure food is cut into very small pieces. Make sure the child sits while eating. Never leave a toddler alone when eating.

Diapering and Toileting

Infants frequently need their diapers changed. Always change a diaper if it's wet or dirty. Check diapers before and after nap time and feeding.

When changing a diaper, first gather all the supplies. These include a clean diaper, wipes, and diaper cream, if used. Place the supplies within reach of the changing area. Lie the baby on a changing table or flat surface. Use a safety restraint if there is one. Keep one hand on the baby. Do not leave the baby unattended. Remove the dirty diaper. Holding the baby's ankles, lift his hips and wipe thoroughly from front to back. Use diaper cream if parents have instructed you to. Properly dispose of the dirty diaper and wash your hands.

Toddlers who have recently learned to use the toilet may need your help in the bathroom. Ask parents what help the child will need. Know what words the toddler says when she needs to use the toilet. Wash the child's hands and your hands after helping a child use the toilet.

What Should You Do?

You're changing a 2-year-old's diaper and there's a knock at the front door. You should:

A Jump up and answer it. It might be important!

B Stay with the child and do not answer the door.

C Ask the 2-year-old's brother to answer the door.

D Quickly run to a window and see who it is.

19

Caring for Preschoolers and School-Age Children

Older children are more independent than infants and toddlers, but they still need your undivided attention. Stay near and watch children carefully. Provide help when they need it, and enjoy your time together.

Feeding

Preschoolers and school-age children vary in the foods they like and how much they eat. Start with small portions. Younger children are often messy eaters. Don't force a child to eat. A lack of interest in food is normal at this age. Preschoolers and school-age children can help with simple meal preparation. Have them help wash fruits and vegetables, put toppings on pizza, or set the table.

Toileting

Some preschoolers may still need help going to the bathroom. A parent will let you know how to handle this.

Sleep

Switch from lively to calming activities about 30 minutes before bedtime. Turn off the TV or computer. Play a quiet game or read bedtime stories. Let the child know about 15 minutes beforehand that bedtime is near. Make sure you follow the child's normal bedtime routine.

Bathing

Babysitters should not give baths to infants. If toddlers or older children need to be bathed, discuss bath-time routine with parents.

Bath-Time Rules

- Never leave a child alone in a bathtub. Children can drown in as little as 1 inch (2.5 centimeters) of water.
- Only fill the tub to a child's hips.
- Water should be warm, but not hot.
- Help the child in and out of the bathtub. It's slippery and he or she may fall.
- Keep the child seated while bathing.

Behavior Basics

There are many reasons children misbehave. A sibling is jealous of his brother or sister. A toddler is hungry, tired, or frustrated. A child wants attention or is bored. Great babysitters know how to deal with behavior problems when they arise or prevent them before they begin.

Encouraging Positive Behavior

A good way to keep behavior flare-ups from ever starting is to encourage positive behavior. Here are a few suggestions:

- Let children know when they've done a good job, such as when they put away their toys or go to bed on time. "Thanks for helping to put the blocks away. Putting toys away is easy when we work together."
- Set reasonable limits and let children know your expectations up front. "We're going to be together until your parents come home. We'll follow the same rules that you use every day."
- Don't favor one child over another.
- Be flexible. Don't force a child to take part in an activity if she doesn't want to play.
- Give advance notice when it's time to change from one activity to another, such as bedtime.
- Give children choices. "Do you want to play a game inside or outside?" If a child wants a soft drink but is not allowed, ask, "Do you want milk or water?"
- Smile and keep a good attitude. Have fun!

Correcting Misbehavior

Correcting misbehavior is one of the most challenging tasks you'll face when babysitting. Discuss with parents in advance how they handle problematic behavior. It's important to stay positive. Let the child know you're unhappy with the behavior, not the child.

You have three choices when faced with misbehavior.

- **Do nothing.** This is a good choice if a child is acting out for attention and not in danger of hurting himself or others.
- Most behavior problems are solved when you **say something.** In a calm voice, explain to the child why her behavior is not acceptable.
- There are times when you need to **use physical action** to control behavior. For example, if a child is about to throw a toy at his baby brother, take the toy away.

Remember!

It is never OK to shake, hit, or verbally insult a child. This is abuse. Shaking a child can cause brain damage and even death. No matter how frustrated you feel, stay calm and don't lose your cool. Take a deep breath. Think about the best way to handle the situation.

What Should You Do?

A 5-year-old refuses to play the game you've suggested. You should:

A Sternly tell the child he must play.
B Wait a few minutes then suggest the same game.
C Send the child to bed without dinner.
D Ask the child what he would prefer to play.

Redirect Behavior

Provide a child with an alternate, approved activity. For
example, if a child is throwing toys indoors, suggest that you
go outside and play catch. If a child begins to draw on the wall,
give him a piece of paper to draw on instead.

Tell children what you want them to do

Instead of "Don't run," tell children, "Walk please." "Roll the ball
on the floor" tells a child what he should do instead of throwing.
"Talk quietly" helps a child to know you want him to lower his voice.

Consequences

Sometimes children need to know that their misbehavior has consequences. The consequence should relate to the behavior. Ask parents about appropriate ways to handle these situations. If a child is throwing blocks, tell him, "Blocks are for building. Please build with them on the floor." If the child continues to throw the blocks, a consequence may be needed. For example, you could put the blocks away and help him find another activity.

What Should You Do?

The 6-year-old you put to bed an hour ago keeps getting up. You should:

A Let her watch TV until she goes to sleep.
B Scold the child and give her a time out.
C Call the child's parents and ask them what to do.
D Calmly return her to bed.

What Should You Do?
Quiz Answers

page 11

C Decline the sleepover invitation and go to your babysitting job.

Stay professional and keep your commitments.

page 19

B Stay with the child and do not answer the door.

Never leave a young child alone. If there is an emergency and you must leave the bedroom, finish dressing the child and take him with you.

page 25

D Ask the child what he would prefer to play.

Be flexible. Never force a child to do an activity he doesn't want to do. Suggest an alternative activity. Or ask the child what he would like to do. It could also be that the child is tired, hungry, or not feeling well. Try to find out.

page 27

D Calmly return the child to bed.

Be kind, but firmly stick to the child's normal sleep routine. Try reading a story, playing an imaginary game, or listening to soft music.

Bonus Questions!

The preschooler you're babysitting starts to hit his sister. You should first:

A Calmly separate the children.
B Yell at him to stop.
C Do nothing. Let them work it out themselves.
D Yank the preschooler by the arm and send him to his room.

A First, separate the children. If the other child has been hurt, comfort her and take care of any injuries she may have. Then react calmly to the child who has done the hitting. Tell him it's not OK to hurt someone else when he's angry.

A 5-year-old starts throwing her toy blocks around the room. You should:

A Take her toys away.
B Talk to her about her behavior then redirect her to a more acceptable activity.
C Put her in a timeout until she calms down.
D Punish her by taking away her TV privileges.

B Children don't always understand how their behavior affects others. You might say, "When you throw your blocks, you might hurt yourself or someone else." Then redirect her to another activity.

Glossary

alternate (AWL-tuhr-net)—one of an option of things from which to choose

client (KLY-uhnt)—a customer

communication (kuh-myoo-nuh-KAY-shuhn)—the sharing of facts, ideas, or feelings with other people

consequence (KAHN-suh-kwentz)—the result of an action

independent (in-di-PEN-duhnt)—free from the control of other people or things

infant (IN-fent)—a child under the age of 1

interview (IN-tur-vyoo)—to ask someone questions to find out more about something

routine (roo-TEEN)—a regular way or pattern of doing tasks

toddler (TOD-lur)—a between the ages of 1 and 3

Read More

Babysitting Secrets: Everything You Need to Have a Successful Babysitting Business. San Francisco: Chronicle Books, 2012.

Bondy, Halley. *Don't Sit on the Baby!* The Ultimate Guide to Sane, Skilled, and Safe Babysitting. San Francisco: Zest Books, 2012.

Moss, Marissa. *Amelia's Guide to Babysitting.* New York: Simon and Schuster, 2008.

Internet Sites

FactHound offers a safe, fun way to find Internet sites related to this book. All of the sites on FactHound have been researched by our staff.

Here's all you do:

Visit *www.facthound.com*

Type in this code: 9781491407646

Check out projects, games and lots more at
www.capstonekids.com

Index